"I Have Decided"

31 Decisions for your Christian Walk

To: Danial

Blessings in Jesus

Love you Brother

-Author Andrew Bullins

"I Have Decided"

31 Decisions for your Christian Walk

By

Andrew Bullins

Published by For His Glory Writing Co.
5792 Lakeshore Drive
Bean Station, TN 37708
www.forhisglorywc.com

Cover Design by Ash Lucero, A to Z Digital Productions

Unless otherwise noted, all Scripture quotations are from the New King James Version of the Bible, Copyright © 1982 by Thomas Nelson.

Scripture quotations identified KJV are from the King James Version of the Bible, Copyright © 1954, 1958, 1962, 1964, 1965, 1987 by The Lockman Foundation.

ISBN: 978-0-578-59002-8
LCCN: 2019951946

Printed in the United States of America.

TABLE OF CONTENTS

I

HAVE

DECIDED

31 DECISIONS FOR YOUR
CHRISTIAN WALK

ANDREW BULLINS

ACKNOWLEDGMENTS

I would like to acknowledge and give honor to my parents Bobby and Barbara Bullins for all of their love and support. Also, my sisters Bobbi jo Pica, Hannah Lima, and Miriam Thompson for all of your encouragement.

I would like to extend a special thank you to my Aunts Mary Ann Ramey, and Nancy Bryant. As well as my "sidekick" Zachary Shelton and Matthew Thompson for sowing your time and resources into the vision.

Lastly, I would like to acknowledge and give thanks to Ash Lucero, Joshua Buchanan, and Charisma Media for the contributions made to support me and this book.

That if you confess with your mouth the Lord Jesus and believe in your heart that God has raised Him from the dead, you will be saved.

Romans 10:9

INTRODUCTION

"I Have Decided to
Follow Jesus."

Life is full of everyday decisions and after we believe in Jesus, this doesn't change. In fact, we still have many decisions that we will have to make in our walk with the Lord. God expects those decisions to be based on His Word, the Bible. The Bible is filled with everyday life situations and the instructions on how to handle them. The instructions in the Bible are the full authority that we should live by.

I love that God has given us free will. He desires a people that choose Him above the world, and He loves us at every turn of truth and mistake, ready to lift us up. Our God came to earth to live as a human so that He could see through our eyes. He is a God who loves through the good and bad decisions. Jesus shed His blood as the perfect sacrifice so that we can find true love, be reconciled to God, and made worthy through the blood.

The reason for this devotional is to apply Scripture to our lives and the decisions we encounter. This devotional is practical and will aid all believers from babes to elders. As you embark on this walk as a Christian, begin intentionally basing each decision you make on the Word of God. Each day-devotional is titled with a decision, and Scripture reference, and concludes with a declaration and interactive activity.

DAY 1

"I Have Decided to Use the Armor of God."

Finally, my brethren, be strong in the Lord and in the power of His might. Put on the whole armor of God, that you may be able to stand against the wiles of the devil. For we do not wrestle against flesh and blood, but against principalities, against powers, against the rulers of the darkness of this age, against spiritual hosts of wickedness in the heavenly places. Therefore take up the whole armor of God, that you may be able to withstand in the evil day, and having done all, to stand.

Stand therefore, having girded your waist with truth, having put on the breastplate of righteousness, and having shod your feet with the preparation of the gospel of peace; above all, taking the shield of faith with which you will be able to quench all the fiery darts of the wicked one. And take the helmet of salvation, and the sword of the Spirit, which is the word of God; praying always with all prayer and supplication in the Spirit, being watchful to this end with all perseverance and supplication for all the saints—

Ephesians 6:10-18

In order to properly fight and wage war in the Spirit, we must understand that we have armor and weapons that the Lord has given us. Many times we feel like we are fighting a losing battle, but maybe it is because we aren't fully dressed! God has given us every weapon and the protection we need to fight in the spirit realm, but if you have just one piece of armor, you are not prepared for battle.

Look at it like this: if you are a soldier going into a Medieval battle with only a helmet, it is not going to end well for you. What would protect the rest of your body? What would you fight with? Even if you had just a sword, would that be enough? No, you would be open to sustaining bodily injuries.

We cannot walk this Christian life fully until we realize what the Lord has given us to use each day for victory.

Here is what the Lord has given us:

- <u>Truth</u>: The garment or belt that encircles and surrounds your waist that secures you.
- <u>Righteousness</u>: The breastplate that covers the chest cavity and protects one of your most vital organs, your heart.

- Gospel: Shod or place on your feet the shoes of peace and stand without fear because you are firmly planted and protected on your path by the word of God.
- Faith: When you are under siege take refuge in your faith in God, raise your shield that will further protect your body from attack, your body is God's vessel to be used in the earth.
- Salvation: The helmet protects another major organ and that is your brain which is a part of the nervous system and coordinates all of your movements.
- Spirit/Word of God: Take hold of the sword which has been placed in your hands and possession as a means of power, authority, and honor to strike back at the enemy and grab a hold of all that God has for you.

It is critical that we understand the verb tenses of these verses that deal with the armor of God. Notice in verses 14 and 15 that the verbs are in the past tense "having." But the verbs in verses 16 and 17 are in the present tense "taking" and "take." The idea is that the first 3 pieces of armor (the belt of truth, the breastplate of righteousness, and the shoes of the gospel of peace) are pieces that should remain on us at all times. That is, we should be always surrounded with the truth of God's Word, we should always know and understand our righteous standing before God, and we should always know that we are at peace with God (Rom. 5:1).

The last 3 pieces of armor (the shield, helmet, and sword) are weapons that we need to pick up ("take") at the start of every battle.

Notice that each weapon can be used both offensively and defensively. Notice also that there is no piece of armor that protects the back. Retreating in battle will destroy you.

<u>Make this your declaration today</u>: "I have decided to take and use every piece of armor that the Lord has given me, and I will live a victorious life in Jesus' name!"

Thought and Reflection:

1. Take the time today to prayerfully put on every piece of armor, one by one.

NOTES

NOTES

DAY 2

"I Have Decided to Walk in the Spirit and Not in the Flesh."

I say then: Walk in the Spirit, and you shall not fulfill the lust of the flesh.

Galatians 5:16

Scripture tells us that we should walk in the Spirit and not in the flesh. The flesh is the part of us that is dominated by sin. This is why the Bible instructs us to crucify our flesh, which means to die daily of our fleshly, human desires. Galatians 5 verses 24 and 25 says, "And those who are Christ's have crucified the flesh with its passions and desires. If we live in the Spirit, let us also walk in the Spirit."

The reason for this is so we don't fall into temptation and iniquity (sin). The enemy would love nothing more than to have you get up every morning and live in the flesh; his job is to pull you away from God's truth and purpose in your life.

According to Ephesians 4:22-24, we are putting off the old self that was led by deceitful desires and putting on the new self which is made in true righteousness and holiness like our creator. We all face different lusts that our flesh desires, and sometimes we encounter them daily. When we walk in the Spirit, we can see how the enemy has set up devices throughout the day to use against us and our testimony. We must react with God's word through the Holy Spirit.

Make this declaration today: "I have decided to walk fully in the Spirit and power of God. Flesh you are under subjection to the Spirit! I will submit my life to the Holy Spirit, and I refuse to be dominated by sin in any area of my life."

Thought and Reflection:

1. What are some of the things you face throughout the day?
    List on one side the fleshly thoughts and on the other
    spiritual thoughts.

    This will help you get a better understanding of what
    thoughts, actions, and reactions you need to work on to
    help you walk better in the Spirit.

NOTES

_____

_____

_____

_____

_____

NOTES

DAY 3

"I Have Decided to Step into God's Call."

For the gifts and the calling of God are irrevocable.

Romans 11:29

One of the most prominent questions I hear Christians ask is, "How do I know what God's calling is on my life?" We all have heard the famous slogan, "If God calls you, then He equips you." Well, that's easier said than done, to be honest, right? But the root of it is true. God does have everything you need available. The key is your YES. When you say, "Yes," that gives God a willing vessel for Him to work with.

God does not call the qualified–He qualifies the called. Or, to put it another way, God is not looking for ability; He is looking for availability. See, God is waiting on you to simply say, "Yes," and HE will do the rest. Could you imagine the difference you would see in your life, your family's lives and community if you would just say, "Yes," to the call? It's never too late! Imagine what answering the call to prayer would do for your family. Imagine what answering the call to evangelize would do for your neighborhood or workplace.

Go For It!

Make this declaration today: "I have decided to step into God's call in my life today. I will say, "Yes," to obey every command in Scripture that comes to my mind, and I will say, "Yes," to every prompting of His Spirit."

Thought and Reflection

Take time today to think about your passions and purpose.

1. Make a list of the things you are good at. This could be a gifting, talent, or ability as well as any of your passions.

2. Now, put your faith to work by making a list of two short term goals that relate to your purpose or passion that you can begin pursuing today.

   An example could be if you are a writer and want to start a blog, start with a goal of journaling 30 minutes per day, and set a goal to research 10 minutes a day the topic "how to start a blog" to begin those first steps of creating an action plan behind your pursuit.

NOTES

NOTES

DAY 4

"I Have Decided to Walk in God's Love"

Create in me a clean heart, O God,
And renew a steadfast spirit within me.

Psalms 51:10

Are you walking in God's love? The reason we have to walk in love is because that's what the world needs. People do not care how much we know until they know how much we care. When the world around us sees the love we have for each other, and for them, then we will see true change.

God's love is a free gift; we freely receive the love of God and freely give to others. Love is not only a noun but a verb, meaning love requires action. When you truly begin walking in the love of God the fruit of your actions will also line up accordingly. 1

Corinthians 13 is the blueprint of how you can begin walking in the love of God daily. Ask the Lord to search your heart and fill the spaces that you need to love and be loved.

Make this declaration today: "I have decided to walk in God's love. No matter how others treat me, the love that God showed me, I will show to others."

Thought and Reflection:

1. Read, meditate, and write down the scripture 1 Corinthians 13.

2. Describe a past situation that you haven't been the best example of love. Perhaps it was when your boss was unreasonably critical. Or maybe it was when your spouse came home in a bad mood. Or possibly when your children were acting out of line.

3. How would love be properly displayed in the past situation you have described above?

NOTES

_____

_____

_____

NOTES

DAY 5

"I Have Decided to Guard my Tongue."

Death and life are in the power of the tongue,
And those who love it will eat its fruit.

Proverbs 18:21

Many situations arise that we can control with our tongue—or at least use our tongues to bring peace (words or no words). Did you know that we should choose our words wisely? Speaking love is the most powerful thing we can do in any situation; our flesh doesn't always want to speak love. If we decided to speak life into every situation, we would save ourselves a lot of drama, shame, stress, and heartache.

You have the power to speak life back into dead situations. We can't take back words, but we can start to speak words of life where we once spoke death.

Have you ever said, "Shame on you!" or perhaps, "You'll never amount to anything!" You can reverse those words of death by declaring blessings upon the people who spoke those words. Jesus told us to, "bless those who curse you and pray for those who despitefully use you" (Luke 6:28). Bless their jobs, their families, their marriages, etc. This will keep you from bitterness and resentment. You cannot be bitter against someone that you are actively blessing. Decide today to speak life to yourself, family, coworkers, and friends.

Make this declaration today: "I have decided to guard my tongue today. I will proactively speak words of life to everyone, and no matter how people may treat me, I will react with words of life and not death."

Thought and Reflection:

1. Think about a situation you didn't speak life into and write it down? Maybe you chose the wrong words from a place of anger.

2. If you had the chance, what would you say today?

3. Now, say it aloud! Speak life and resurrect the dead situations in your life today.

NOTES

NOTES

DAY 6

"I Have Decided to Be a Light."

That you may become blameless and harmless, children of God without fault in the midst of a crooked and perverse generation, among whom you shine as lights in the world.

Philippians 2:15

In a dark room, a single spark of light can be seen, and our eyes are drawn to that single flicker of light. Church, this is how you are in this world. You may not always feel that you are shining, but you are. Be the Light that this world needs—the light that people need to bring them hope; This hope is anchored in Christ, and His light consumes the darkness.

As darkness gets darker, your light has to get brighter. You have been shining the unstoppable light of Christ and leading the way for the future Church. You have to shine and shine you will. Our lights are to shine upon Jesus, and not on ourselves. "Let your light so shine before men that they may see your good works and glorify your Father in heaven" (Matthew 5:16).

Make this declaration today: "I have decided to be a light today. No matter the darkness around me, I will shine my light. I will not hide it under a bushel, but shine it brightly that my Father in heaven may be glorified."

Thought and Reflection:

When the atmosphere of a room is heavy with tension, let your light of the joy of the Lord shine brightly. When a situation arises that most people would explode in anger, shine the light of the Lord's forgiveness in the situation.

1. What area in your life needs the light you carry? This can be a situation, a place or a person.

2. Explain what the Lord has done for you, and how He can do it for others.

NOTES

_____

_____

_____

NOTES

DAY 7

"I Have Decided to Bring My First Fruits."

Honor the Lord with your possessions,
And with the firstfruits of all your increase.

Proverbs 3:9

Scripture tells us to bring our first fruits to the Lord—the first of everything we have prospered. As we prosper in this life, God uses our finances, talents, gifts, and skills to build the kingdom and to edify each believer.

Scripture tells us that God honored Abel's sacrifice. Abel offered the firstborn (first fruits) of his flock and of their fat (Gen. 4:4). Do we offer the Lord our first fruits, or what is left over?

Don't get in the rut of not giving, because the spirit of generosity breaks the spirit of poverty in the kingdom. Giving your finances breaks the spirit of poverty and debt in the kingdom. Giving your talents, such as teaching, breaks spiritual ignorance in the kingdom.

Giving your time is a benefit for you and others because there are many positive outcomes spiritually, mentally, and physically that are gained for both the giver and the receiver. You know the saying and biblical principle, "You reap what you sow" (Gal 6:7-9). When you give it will be given back to you (Luke 6:38).

Make this declaration today: "I have decided to bring my first fruits to God today. I will put God first in all my life: my finances, time, talents, and more."

Thought and Reflection

1. Think about all of the things you spend money on that are luxuries, or things you really don't need. How could that money be used to benefit others?

NOTES

_____

_____

_____

_____

_____

_____

NOTES

DAY 8

"I Have Decided to Have One Heart."

---

then I will give them one heart and one way, that they may fear Me forever, for the good of them and their children after them.

Jeremiah 32:39

The Church is referred to as ONE body in Scripture. If we are compared to a body, then we have to have a heart, right? God has connected all believers' hearts, knitting them together through the blood of Jesus. The heart inside your body needs to have adequate blood and electrical conduction to beat in a normal rhythm. If that rhythm gets outside of normal, then dysfunction within the body will happen.

The heart also supplies perfusion (rate of blood flow) to the body, just as the blood of Jesus supplies the church with power and love. Adequate perfusion is necessary to evaluate a person's body color, temperature, and overall condition (such as swollen, sunken, dry, soft, firm, etc.) It is our life supply.

In like manner, there must be an adequate flow of the Spirit in order for the body of Christ to function properly; and there must be a proper flow of the Spirit in our own individual lives in order for us to maintain spiritual health. We must beat in rhythm within our lives (with the Holy Spirit) to bring change, and that rhythm is LOVE and UNITY!

Make this declaration today: I have decided to guard my heart with all diligence. I will also make every effort to maintain one heart in the body of Christ.

Thought and Reflection:

Think of ways you can begin promoting unity and love as a Christian. Perhaps you can begin serving at your local church, or volunteer your time at a soup kitchen, or donate to a local non-profit dedicated to serving your community.

NOTES

NOTES

DAY 9

"I Have Decided to be Free From Fear."

For God has not given us a spirit of fear, but of power and of love and of a sound mind.

2 Timothy 1:7

Fear is a funny thing. Sometimes it's there and we don't even recognize it. Fear can stop us from stepping into God's call, or not to share our faith, keep us in bed, and live under bondage. God has set us free from all fear (Rom. 8:15), but do we believe it?

Fear is one of the enemy's biggest weapons against us. It brings doubt, shame, and anxiety because fear makes us worry. When a believer is in fear, we are OUT of God's peace and rest. Fear will cause you to act out of emotions and not God's will. If the enemy can corner you with fear, he will paralyze you with it—until you realize you can take authority over the fear. How many times do we make decisions that are based on fear? Fear is the reason many still walk in bondage in the kingdom. Fear keeps you in relationships, jobs, and situations God never intended you to be.

One way to help you in these areas is to first trust God's Word. He tells us in 2 Timothy 1:7, that He has not given us the spirit of fear, but has given us the spirit of love, power, and a sound mind. I don't know about you, but I would rather operate out of love, power, and a sound mind.

Operating out of fear is operating in an unsound mind. It makes us see things that are usually not reality. When the disciples saw Jesus walking to them on the sea, they became afraid and thought that they were seeing a ghost (Matt. 14:26).

So, "Fear be Gone in Jesus' name!"

Make this declaration today: I have decided to refuse fear and worry. Fear has no place in my life. I will trust the Lord to work in my life and my circumstances. And every time that fear will try to rise, I will immediately rebuke it in Jesus' name.

48

Thought and Reflection:

1. What are some of the things you fear?

    Do you fear man's opinion(s) of you? Do you fear the
    unknown future? Write them down and expose the fears
    and proclaim love, power, and a sound mind over them in
    Jesus' name.

NOTES

_____

_____

_____

_____

_____

NOTES

DAY 10

"I Have Decided to Be Still."

Be still and know that I am God. I will be exalted among the nations, I will be exalted in the earth.

Psalm 46:10

Stillness—we all want more of that, right? It would be nice, but sometimes our busy lives don't allow it. So, why does God say to be still if He knows we live in un-still times?

The Biblical definition of "still" is to stop motion or agitation; to restain or make quiet. The reason God wants us to be still is so we can trust Him and hear Him. Does that mean we just lie in our beds in physical stillness? NO! But He does want us to take time out of each day, calm our minds and bodies, and just be still with Him.

This gives us a spiritual recharge, a focus on who God is, and enables us to be more plugged into hearing his voice. When our minds are stimulated with too much thought, worry, and anxiety, we can't hear what God is trying to tell us. When we still our minds, we allow the peace of God to calm us.

Let me illustrate. If you would take a clear glass out of the cupboard and fill it with tap water, the water in that clear glass would look cloudy. But if you would set that same glass of cloudy water on the counter, leave it to remain still for a few minutes, the water will turn crystal clear. In like manner, our minds become cloudy because of the busyness of life, and it is necessary for us to be still before the Lord in order to hear His voice. The more that we remain still before the Lord, the more clearly we will be able to hear His voice speaking to us.

BE STILL AND LET GOD SPEAK!

Make this declaration today: I have decided to be still before the Lord. I will remain still until I can focus my heart and mind upon Him and hear His voice as He speaks to me.

Thought and Reflection:

1. Think about your day. What time can you set aside to be still with God?

2. **_Assignment:_** For the next 7 days take 15 mins and be still.

   I would encourage you to make these 15 minutes the same time every day—it is a time-slot with a purpose—time to be still before the Lord. After the 15 minutes, write down your thoughts and what you believe God is saying each day. As the days go on, you will hear and write more.

   This is called journaling. It is also something that you can look back upon at a later date and see how God met with you, answered your prayers, etc.

Day 1:

Day 2:

Day 3:

Day 4:

Day 5:

Day 6:

Day 7:

NOTES

_____

_____

_____

_____

_____

_____

_____

NOTES

DAY 11

"I Have Decided to Listen, Trust, and Act."

Now an angel of the Lord spoke to Philip, saying, "Arise and go toward the south along the road which goes down from Jerusalem to Gaza." This is desert. So he arose and went. And behold, a man of Ethiopia, a eunuch of great authority under Candace the queen of the Ethiopians, who had charge of all her treasury, and had come to Jerusalem to worship, was returning. And sitting in his chariot, he was reading Isaiah the prophet. Then the Spirit said to Philip, "Go near and overtake this chariot."

So Philip ran to him, and heard him reading the prophet Isaiah, and said, "Do you understand what you are reading?"

And he said, "How can I, unless someone guides me?" And he asked Philip to come up and sit with him. The place in the Scripture which he read was this:

*"He was led as a sheep to the slaughter;
And as a lamb before its shearer is silent,
So He opened not His mouth.*

In His humiliation His justice was taken away,
And who will declare His generation?
For His life is taken from the earth."

So the eunuch answered Philip and said, "I ask you, of whom does the prophet say this, of himself or of some other man?" Then Philip opened his mouth, and beginning at this Scripture, preached Jesus to him. Now as they went down the road, they came to some water. And the eunuch said, "See, here is water. What hinders me from being baptized?"

Then Philip said, "If you believe with all your heart, you may."

And he answered and said, "I believe that Jesus Christ is the Son of God."

So he commanded the chariot to stand still. And both Philip and the eunuch went down into the water, and he baptized him. Now when they came up out of the water, the Spirit of the Lord caught Philip away, so that the eunuch saw him no more; and he went on his way rejoicing.

Acts 8:26-39

Have you heard the Holy Spirit tell you to do something, and you didn't do it? You may have even questioned if it was the Holy Spirit? Let me help you with something. We see in Scripture that Phillip was led by the Spirit to where the eunuch was. As Philip ministered to the eunuch, he (the eunuch) got saved, baptized, and took the gospel back with him to Ethiopia.

Because Phillip listened, trusted and acted upon what the Spirit told him to do, the eunuch got saved, and we don't know and only God knows how many lives were impacted by the eunuch taking the gospel back to his country of Ethiopia. Don't think about your missed opportunities to share the gospel. Make the decision now to start fresh and listen, trust, and act.

Listen: Listen to what the Spirit is saying.
Trust: What the Spirit is saying.
Act: Do what the Spirit is telling you to do.

Delayed obedience is a brother to disobedience. How do we know if it is the Holy Spirit speaking or the devil speaking? We know if it is something to do with the gospel going forward, then it's not the devil telling you to do it.

Make this declaration today: I have decided to keep a listening ear to the Holy Spirit. I will trust what the Spirit says, and I will act upon it.

NOTES

_____

_____

_____

_____

_____

_____

NOTES

DAY 12

"I Have Decided to be Crushed and Pressed."

You prepare a table before me in the presence of my enemies; You anoint my head with oil; my cup runs over.

Psalm 23:5

Now, I know that title sounds harsh. Wow! Crushed and pressed? Who wants that to happen to them? Well, to be honest, we all should. When I say crushed and pressed, it must take place in the Spirit.

In biblical times, in order to bring forth olive oil, they would place the olives in the olive press trough and roll a millstone over the olives. Olives are half their weight in oil. Looking at one, you would never guess that. As the stone rolled over the olives, it would crush the olive and press it to extract the oil, and separate the skin and the flesh of the olive. The skin would go into a basket and the oil into basins. This was the first and purest oil. Then the farmers would take the skins from the basket, put them back into the press, and extract the last remaining oil they could get.

When it looks like there is nothing left in your life to be used, think about the olive oil process. Let the Lord crush and press you to bring forth an anointing oil for his glory, and get rid of what is not needed. He can bring forth oil out of every area of our lives if we allow him. He isn't finished with us yet!

Make this declaration today: I have decided to allow the Lord to crush and press me. I will submit myself to His crushing, allow Him to discard anything that does not glorify Him and to be pressed that His anointing may flow through my life.

Thought and Reflection:

As the Lord crushes and presses us in the Spirit, it exposes the things that we need to get rid of that is not of Him.

1. What are the things in your life that could be holding you back from oil being produced in your life?

NOTES

_____

_____

_____

_____

_____

_____

NOTES

DAY 13

"I Have Decided to Declutter."

But seek first the kingdom of God and His righteousness, and all these things shall be added to you.

Matthew 6:33

Do you ever feel like there is just too much stuff in your life physically? I do! When we have our minds occupied on so much stuff, or have our houses, bedrooms, or space where we reside the most full of un-useful things; it can keep our minds cluttered and anxiety starts to set in.

When Samuel tried to introduce Saul as king to the Israelites, Saul could not be found. The reason? I Samuel 10:22 tells us that it was because "he hath hid himself among the stuff" (KJV). Often, the reason why many people have so much "stuff" is because they are hiding behind it. They try to "keep up with the Jones'" thinking that such "stuff" will bring them satisfaction; but the truth is, the more that we own, the more it owns us.

When we declutter our lives, we free our minds of extra clutter, and this allows us to regain focus, clear our minds, and listen. Today, start a declutter process of your life. Maybe you have your closet full of stuff that you don't even need? Perhaps you have been meaning to clean it out, but haven't taken the step.

Decluttering needs to take place both in the spiritual as well as the natural. We need to declutter spiritually by getting back to the basics—studying the Scriptures and prayer. We need to declutter in the natural by refusing to buy things that we don't need, and getting rid of things that we don't use. This will free us spiritually and practically.

See how "stuff" takes up space in our minds? Seek first the kingdom, and God will supply all you need.

Make this declaration today: I have decided to declutter my life today that I will not be distracted from serving my Lord. I will go back and concentrate on the basics of Bible study and prayer. I will also refrain from the temptations to buy things that I really do not need and get rid of things that I never use.

Thought and Reflection:

1. **Assignment**: What clutter do you have in your living space? I have found that when I decluttered, my mind and spirit have become freer. Start the process today.

NOTES

_____

_____

_____

_____

_____

_____

_____

NOTES

DAY 14

"I Have Decided to Build my House on the Rock."

Therefore whoever hears these sayings of mine and does them, I will liken him to a wise man who built his house upon a rock: and the rain descended, the floods came, and the winds blew, and beat on that house; and it did not fall, for it was founded on the rock. But everyone who hears these sayings of Mine, and does not do them, will be like a foolish man who built his house on the sand: and the rain descended, the floods came, and the winds blew and beat on that house; and it fell. And great was its fall.

Matthew 7:24-27

In the Bible, we find physical comparisons to help us understand a spiritual lesson. The times in which we live, things are always shifting. People are continually looking for satisfaction and the next best thing. The world offers so many temptations that speak to our flesh. People in the world and even some Christians are being tossed to and fro in every direction, and have built their houses on shifting sands.

Imagine standing on sand, how it moves, how it throws you off balance easily, how it blows in the wind, and shifts in every direction. Also, you never know how deep you can sink. Now imagine standing on a solid rock and how easy it is to maintain balance, and walk without worry of sinking. Rocks can withstand wind, storms, and rains. But each of those things moves sand into whatever direction they are going.

Believe it or not, there are people who can tell if your house is built on sand or rock, and they will take advantage of the sand-builders, because they are not stable, and believe whatever comes their way. Build your house on the Rock, and it shall not be moved.

How to build your life on the Rock:

- Build your life on a firm foundation—read Scripture and apply it to your life daily.
- Faith—trust Jesus for every decision that you make.
- Prayer—pray about everything.
- Relationship—Jesus is our Rock.

<u>Make this declaration today:</u> I have decided to build my life on the Rock of my salvation, the Lord Jesus Christ. Every surface or doctrine that causes me to slip or drift away from the Lord I will reject, that my life may be firmly planted upon the Rock.

Thought and Reflection:

Think and act in terms of relationship with the Lord. When we walk with him, we won't be moved. As we can see in our verses above, the difference between the wise man and the foolish man is in the doing. Both the wise man and the foolish man heard the sayings of Jesus, but the wise man "does them," and the foolish man "does not do them." It is much easier to do something for someone you love than it is to do it simply because you know that it is the right thing to do.

1. **Assignment**: Write what areas are rock in your life. What words of Jesus are you doing?

2. What areas are sand in your life? These are areas that you know what to do, but you are not doing them. Sample areas could be maintaining a regular prayer life, faithful Bible study, telling others about Christ, etc.

NOTES

DAY 15

"I Have Decided to Extend Grace."

And He said to me, "My grace is sufficient for you, for My strength is made perfect in weakness.

2 Corinthians 12:9

We all have those times in our lives when we can choose or not choose to extend grace or act out of the flesh. As Christians, we carry the purest and most potent form of love in all of the universe—which is grace. The form of grace that we as believers will extend in situations is goodwill and kindness. Grace is a gift from God, and as His children, we are to extend that same grace in our lives.

God doesn't always expect us to keep to ourselves the gifts He has given us, but to take them, and bless the world and each other. Even as believers there are many times and situations that we experience issues extending grace; for instance, when we have been hurt or feel like we have been wronged. However, our emotions do not exempt us from showing grace. Trust me, I know it is hard in some situations. I went through a very painful relationship experience a few years ago. Feelings of hurt and betrayal can definitely make you second guess extending grace, but God calls us to a higher standard, and that standard is Jesus.

Jesus went through a similar situation; He experienced every temptation and trial that we might find ourselves. Judas betrayed Him, Peter denied Him 3 times, His enemies lied about Him and crucified Him. And yet, He is still offering grace. Hebrews 4:16 says, "Let us therefore come boldly to the throne of grace, that we may obtain mercy and find grace to help in time of need." His throne is a throne of grace. Can people say that about our lives? Can they say that every time they approach us, they may obtain mercy and find grace to help in time of need? Always think, how would Jesus react?

So, to the waitress who gets your order wrong; extend grace. To the driver with road rage; extend grace. To the Person who takes "your" parking spot; extend grace. To your family, friends, and co-workers; remember to extend grace!

Make this declaration today: I have decided to extend grace to everyone I contact today. I want people to feel "safe" around me because they can trust that that which comes from me is mercy and grace, and not a judgmental attitude.

Thought and Reflection:

1. What situations have you had a hard time extending grace?

2. Now, how would you display grace and mercy in those situations?

NOTES

NOTES

DAY 16

"I Have Decided to Let God Search Me."

Search me, O God, and know my heart; try me, and know my anxieties; And see if there is any wicked way in me, and lead me in the way everlasting.

Psalm 139:23, 24

God knows more about us than we know about ourselves, and He knows us more than anyone on the planet knows us. We are all different, made beautiful in His image; some are guarded, and others wear their hearts on their sleeves. It's hard for some to open up, even to the one who knows all about us.

In the Psalms, King David cries out for God to search him and know his heart. Why would David ask God to do these things if He already knows? God wants us to trust Him and talk with Him about all things. How can we hear what God wants, if we have our guard up that keeps us from hearing what He is saying?

When we ask God to search us and know us, we are giving his Spirit permission to reveal the things in our hearts that need to be exposed. When you let God search you, you will learn more about yourself than you have ever imagined—things you didn't even know.

I don't know about you, but I love it when God reveals to me things He loves about me, things that I need to work on, and things I didn't even know were there. As God searches us, it allows us to find strength through Him and rely on Him to clean up the messes we have made in our lives.

This searching of God is two-fold. First, it reveals the sin in our lives. "Search me, O God . . . And see if there is any wicked way in me." Second, it lead us into righteousness. "Search me, O God . . . And lead me in the way everlasting" (Psalms 139:23-24).

Search us Oh GOD!

Make this declaration today: I have decided to let the Lord search and know me this day. May His searching reveal things in my life that need to be removed, and may His knowledge of me lead in the way that I need to live.

Thought and Reflection:

1. Pray and ask God to search and reveal to you the things in your heart throughout the day and write them down as you receive revelation.

NOTES

_____

_____

_____

_____

_____

_____

_____

NOTES

DAY 17

"I Have Decided
Not to Covet."

You shall not covet your neighbor's house; you shall not covet your neighbor's wife, nor his male servant, nor his female servant, nor his ox, nor his donkey, nor anything that is your neighbor's.

Exodus 20:17

The biblical meaning of Covet means to desire inordinately; to desire that which it is unlawful to obtain or possess; in a bad sense. As God's children, He wants to give you good and perfect gifts (James 1:17). As the definition above states, coveting another's possessions is not good. Let's face the facts, we all at some point have looked at others and their possessions and thought, "I would like to have that car, house, job, etc."

Sometimes we do this and don't even catch ourselves thinking these thoughts. The reason God steers us away from that is because just a simple thought of wanting what someone else has can lead us down a path of envy and allow jealousy to take root in our hearts. As we start to desire the things of others, we lose grip on what God has blessed us with, and all of a sudden, it's not good enough. We are not thankful, and we think others possessions and gifts become better than what we have been given.

As a result, we begin to position our hearts away from thankfulness and praise, to envy and jealousy. All of a sudden, we begin to work for things God doesn't intend on us having. We go further into debt and even try to operate in another Christian's giftings and callings. Don't lose sight of what God has blessed you with, because you are too busy looking at others. "Godliness with contentment is great gain" (I Tim. 6:6). Godliness alone is not enough. We must be content with what the Lord has blessed us with and not look at others. Life is so much more fulfilling when we have the time to do what God is telling us to do—when we wake up every morning with gratitude for what our Father has given us.

Make this declaration today: I have decided not to covet that which does not belong to me. I will not be envious of anything that someone else may have. I will be grateful for every blessing that the Lord has given me.

Thought and Reflection:

There is an old hymn that begins, "Count your many blessings, name them one by one. Count your many blessings, see what God has done." When our focus is on what others have been blessed with, we will lose sight of what the Lord has blessed us with.

1. Take time today to literally count your blessings, list as many blessings that you can write throughout the day and profess your gratitude to the Lord throughout the day.

When you crank your car (no matter if its a clunker), be thankful. Position your heart to receive all that the Lord has for you in Jesus' name (Hebrews 13:5-6).

NOTES

DAY 18

"I Have Decided to be a Willing Vessel."

And I also heard the voice of the Lord, saying, "Whom shall I send, and who will go for Us?"

Isaiah 6:8

How do I know what God has called me to do? I get asked this question on a daily basis. Many of us have felt that way in our walk. One thing I have learned is that God is just looking for a willing and obedient vessel; someone that will listen and take heed to the instructions He is telling you.

The mistake a lot of us make is that we expect God to do everything and just drop our callings into our laps. God wants us to seek, move, pray, and be willing to be used by Him. If we just sit back, we will never step into our God-given destinies. You have to start somewhere—get involved in your local community, in church activities, etc.

Imagine if the faithful patriarchs and early church never stepped out and said, "Yes," to God? I find it interesting that these patriarchs responded to the "Word of the Lord." The Lord has given us His Word just as He gave a word to the patriarchs. Obeying the Word is the first step to fulfilling your call. Jesus said it best in Luke 2:49, "I must be about my Father's business."

Are you a willing vessel, ready for the Lord to use you in any area of your life? Are you about your Father's business?

Make this declaration today: I have decided to step out in faith to fulfill the Lord's will in my life. I will make the first recorded words of Jesus my motto for the day, "I must be about my Father's business."

Thought and Reflection:

Jesus said in John 7:17, that "if anyone wills to do His will, he shall know." The first step to knowing God's will is always a willing and obedient heart. A vehicle that is moving is always easier to steer than a vehicle that is not.

1. Take some time to reflect: Am I willing to do the things that I know that I should be doing? The more we are willing and obedient to do what we know we should, the more clearly we will hear His voice leading us.

NOTES

NOTES

DAY 19

"I Have Decided to Stand Bold."

Therefore, since we have such hope, we use great boldness of speech.

2 Corinthians 3:12

Boldness means to have courage, bravery, and fearlessness. True boldness that this world and the body of Christ needs comes from the Holy Spirit. God calls us to be bold and to stand strong in HIS truth. Are you standing bold in the truth? Or do you back down when confronted?

Shadrach, Meshach, and Abed-Nego were confronted with a life or death situation. They could have chosen to bow down to the gold image (which would be disobeying God) and live, or they had a choice to obey God and risk their own lives and be put to death. But they boldly proclaimed, "Let it be known, O king, that we do not serve your gods, nor will we worship the gold image which you have set up" (Dan. 3:18). That is boldness!

Sometimes the Lord gives us a word to encourage and uplift, and sometimes it's a word of repentance. It takes boldness to share those things with the people they are intended for. If we don't share, then we are doing people a disservice.

Pray for more boldness—boldness to step into what God is telling you to do. In Acts 4, Peter and John confronted the Sanhedrin. The reaction of the Sanhedrin is remarkable: "Now when they (the Sanhedrin) saw the boldness of Peter and John, and perceived that they were uneducated and untrained men, they marvelled. And they realized that they had been with Jesus" (Acts 4:13). Time spent with Jesus will give you the boldness that you need. Spend time with Him today, receive that needed boldness, and act with that boldness.

Make this declaration today: I have decided to be bold in every circumstance. I will not bow down in compromise, nor will I shy away from the things that I need to do. I will spend time with the Lord that I may gain the boldness that I need in any and every situation.

Thought and Reflection:

1. Describe a situation that put you in an uncomfortable position recently.

    Perhaps you were asked to sing a solo at church, or maybe you were around a group of non-believers and God told you to approach this group and share the good news of the gospel.

2. What were your initial reactions? Did you react with boldness or were you timid? Were you obedient to God in this instance?

3. How can you begin walking in the boldness of the Holy Spirit?

NOTES

NOTES

DAY 20

"I Have Decided to go to Church."

Nor forsaking the assembling of ourselves together, as is the manner of some, but exhorting one another, and so much the more as you see the Day approaching.

Hebrews 10:25

God calls us to congregate together, sing together, and edify one another. Have you ever wondered why so many professing believers haven't found it important to be rooted in their local church expression? Why are so many in the body disconnected? Now, you may attend church every time there is an event or service, but do we really know the importance of it? If God is calling us to attend, then shouldn't our hearts be in it?

Church is good for us. In Psalm 73:2, Asaph tells us of his personal struggles with life. "But as for me, my feet had almost stumbled, my steps had nearly slipped. For I was envious of the boastful, when I saw the prosperity of the wicked." Have you ever felt like that? Asaph went on to say, "When I thought how to understand this, it was too painful for me—UNTIL I WENT INTO THE SANCTUARY OF GOD; then I understood their end" (Ps 73:16, 17). Going to church has a way of refocusing our direction and understanding the big, eternal picture.

Church is good for others when you go. If you could see in the Spirit what takes place when we come together, you would see things that you didn't even know about. You would see the struggling addict (who has just started attending) getting encouragement from your smile. You would hear that one person beside you who never sings because they are shy, burst out in a song because you singing made them know that they can also. You would see that the hug you just gave someone, softened their heart to love again. But most importantly you would see God getting the glory for the love he has bestowed on His people.

Don't think that going to church is something you just do; it is more than that. If you're not planted in a local body of believers, I encourage you to find one. You will never know the impact it will make on your life and the lives of others when you make the decision to go to church.

Make this declaration today: I have decided to go to church whenever possible. I know that I need the church and the church needs me.I will not only go, but I will proactively be a blessing to the people that I meet.

Thought and Reflection:

1. Do you attend church regularly? If no, what has kept you from going?

2. If yes, what has kept you going?

NOTES

NOTES

DAY 21

"I Have Decided to Use and Expand my Gifts."

A man's gift makes room for him, and brings him before great men.

Proverbs 18:16

Everyone in the kingdom of God has been given gifts and talents to be used for the glory of God, to touch lives all around. Are we using our God-given gifts fully for the Lord?

Proverbs 18:16 states that our gifts will make room for us. That tells me that the gift will be as big as we make room for it in our lives. How big and how small your gifting is, truly depends on you and what you desire in your life. God wants us to operate in the giftings He has given us. We do the world a disservice if we don't.

Matthew 25:14-30 reveals the parable of the talents. Three individuals were given a measure of talent(s), "to each one according to his ability" (Matt. 25:15). Two of the three used their talents and were wonderfully rewarded. The one who buried his talent was sternly rebuked by the Lord and suffered eternal consequences.

Make this declaration today: "I have decided to be a good steward of the gifts and talents that God gave me. With the Lord's help, I will bring an increase. Lord, please forgive me for any talents that I have buried in the past. I dig it up today to be used for the glory of God."

Thought and Application:

1. Have you made room for your gift?

    Write down an area of your life that you could utilize your gift to help others.

NOTES

NOTES

Day 22

"I Have Decided to be a Matthew."

As Jesus passed on from there, He saw a man named Matthew sitting at the tax office. And He said to him, "Follow Me." So he arose and followed Him.

Matthew 9:9

Ok, I know the title sounds weird, but follow me on this: When Jesus was picking out His 12 disciples, he came upon Matthew, a tax collector, sitting and doing his job. Jesus went up to Matthew and said, "Follow Me." And Matthew got immediately up and followed Jesus.

What I love about Matthew's story is that he asked no questions. He didn't say, "Wait, I need to finish my shift." He got right up and followed Jesus. Matthew knew that as Jesus spoke those words, that they had power and caused such an immediate shift in his life. He had no other option than to get up and move.

Some of us have met that love and haven't moved yet, even though we have felt the power of God. Luke 14:15-24 contains the story of an invitation to follow Jesus. But the people invited all began to make excuses—"I bought land, and I have to go see it." "I just bought some oxen, and I want to go try them." "I just married a wife." The devil will always help you come up with an excuse to refuse the Lord's invitation to follow and obey Him. We need to recognize this for what they are—empty excuses.

Let's be like Matthew—obey with no questions, and dive right in to follow the love of Jesus today. Leave the old life behind—newness awaits!

<u>Make this declaration today</u>: I have decided to be like Matthew and immediately follow Jesus. I refuse to make or listen to excuses.

Thought and Reflection:

1. Just think of Matthew and all of the 12 disciples for a matter of fact; each of these men were called to leave their current circumstances and lives to follow Him. To be fishers of men. Would you leave it all today to follow Jesus?

2. Think about some areas of your life that God has told you to submit to Him. Perhaps He told you to leave a toxic relationship, or to quit smoking and form healthier habits. How can you begin submitting these areas of your life to Him, and walk in obedience to His will for your life?

NOTES

DAY 23

"I Have Decided Not to Gossip."

Let no corrupt communication proceed out of your mouth, but that which is good to the use of edifying, that it may minister grace unto the hearers.

Ephesians 4:29

Gossip is defined as the sharing of negative information about someone to another person who is not part of the problem or part of the solution. Gossip is something that is easy for anyone to get caught up in. We have to remember as Christians that gossip is a sure way the enemy uses to divide the body and split communities of believers. Gossip can hide itself in many forms: through prayer requests for a person that gives intimate details, through church small groups that hear something about another, and Christians that leave one congregation and go to another because of something they heard that very well may not be true.

Gossip is the root of many church splits, relationship splits, and drama. The Lord intends on the church being drama-free. Gossip violates the commandment, "You shall not murder." It kills relationships and churches. It also violates the commandment, "You shall not steal;" for it steals a person's reputation. When we gossip, we could be spreading lies about a brother or sister in Christ that could do substantial damage to their life. Guard what you say and what you hear, and your heart will remain clean.

We need to take the issue of gossip seriously, because it sows discord among the brethren, and is listed as one of the things that God hates and is an abomination to Him (Prov. 6:16-19). If you have this issue, repent immediately, and ask the Lord to help you.

Make this declaration today: "I have decided to keep my tongue from gossip. I will not share any negative information about someone to anyone who is not part of the problem or part of the solution.

Thought and Reflection:

Gossip can be very damaging to a person's reputation, credibility, and cause severe pain to the people involved.

1. Today, share your heart with the Lord and write down a situation that you engaged in gossip and what you could have done differently.

NOTES

_____

_____

_____

_____

_____

_____

NOTES

DAY 24

"I Have Decided to Give."

For God so loved the world that He GAVE His only begotten Son, that whoever believes in Him should not perish but have everlasting life.

John 3:16

As Christians, we should be the most giving people on earth. Now, I know where our minds go when we hear the word "give". Giving is not always monetary value. There are many ways we can give: love, time, spiritual support, emotional support, monetary, and just being there for others in critical times. What people need the most from you is love, and love will guide your giving. You can give without loving, but you cannot love without giving.

Where would you be today if others had not given to you? God uses other believers to give to us, to pour into us, and it is our job to give back what has been poured into us in Jesus' name.

Listen to the Holy Spirit when He says to give something. Don't listen to the flesh, because it always wants to say no. You will be blessed beyond measure.It is always more blessed to give than to receive (Acts 20:35).

Make this declaration today: I have decided to give generously in all areas of my life. I will make it a point to bless people in every way that I can.

Thought and Reflection:

1. Today, list your giving strengths and weaknesses. This will reveal the feelings you may or may not have about giving, as well as any areas that you may need to improve upon.

2. Next put your faith into action by giving something to someone today as the Spirit leads: perhaps a prayer, a word of encouragement, money, or even a smile.

NOTES

_____

_____

_____

NOTES

DAY 25

"I Have Decided Not to Quench the Spirit."

Do not quench the Spirit.

I Thessalonians 5:19

Have you ever been in a situation and knew the Holy spirit was telling you to do something and you didn't do it? You knew it was Him telling you to speak, to bless a person, testify, or even to shout in church, but you held back? When we do that, we are not obeying what God is telling us to do. We miss out on His blessings, and I don't know about you, but I want everything God has for me.

Remember, the Spirit isn't going to tell you to do anything that is outside His Word, the Bible, so you can trust Him. The next time the

Spirit says to move and do something, that's what you need to do. You will never know what impact you will make in others and your own life when you obey. You may have the words that someone needs to hear that day that will save their life.You may also inspire someone to listen to the Spirit as well.

I encourage you to listen today. You may just be surprised at God!

Make this declaration today: I have decided to not quench what the Spirit wants to do in me and through me. I will listen and obey His promptings upon my heart.

Thought and Reflection:

1. Describe a situation when you knew the Holy spirit was telling you to do something and you didn't do it?

2. List something you did today that was prompted by the Holy Spirit. Describe what happened as a result of your obedience?

NOTES

_____

_____

_____

_____

NOTES

DAY 26

"I Have Decided to Live in Peace."

And the peace of God which surpasses all understanding, will guard your hearts and minds through Christ Jesus.

Philippians 4:7

Scripture tells us that the Lord gives us peace that surpasses all understanding. There are several tools the enemy uses to try and take our peace; I'm going to cover three ways the enemy steals your peace.

Fear: When the enemy brings us fear, it causes us to act out of timidity and distrust, and not peace and faith. I have heard many Christians profess that they have made many decisions because, "they had peace about it." Fear will keep you from making the right decisions that the Lord is leading you to make.

Anxiety: Anxiety is a feeling of uncertainty about a situation or an uncertain outcome. How many of us have felt that way? Scripture tells us that, as long as we seek the kingdom of God first, we have nothing to worry about. If you seek that first, you will find yourself less anxious. Anxiety steals our trust, and we remove ourselves out of the will of God for our lives.

Depression: Depression makes us focus on our emotions, specifically emotions of sadness. Do we have peace when we focus on sadness? No—because there is no sadness in the Lord. He understands what we feel and go through, but He wants us to trust Him through everything, so we can rely on Him. When we rely on the Lord, we will find that the peace is there; we just couldn't see it because we were focused on us. Let depression know that it can't have your peace and joy in Jesus' name.

When we live from peace, we won't face fear, anxiety, and depression as much if we rely on the peace of the Lord. Any time your mind starts the battle, speak out and proclaim that you have the peace that passess all understanding in Jesus' name. When you speak the Word, the enemy flees.

Make this declaration: I have decided to live from the peace that God has given me. I believe that He has given me a peace that goes beyond my circumstances, my future, and even my understanding.

Thought and Reflection:

1. Reflect on a time that you made a decision that you just didn't have peace with? Why did you make the decision at that particular time? Was it because of fear, worry, or anxiety?

2. What if you walked in peace to the best of your ability each day? How would that affect your daily life?

NOTES

_____

_____

_____

NOTES

DAY 27

"I Have Decided to live in my Christ-given Identity."

Do you not know that the unrighteous will not inherit the kingdom of God? Do not be deceived. Neither fornicators, nor idolaters, nor adulterers, nor homosexuals, nor sodomites, nor thieves, nor covetous, nor drunkards, nor revilers, nor extortioners will inherit the kingdom of God. And such were some of you. But you were washed, but you were sanctified, but you were justified in the name of the Lord Jesus and by the Spirit of our God.

I Corinthians 6:9-11

As we grow in our walk, we start to see the changes that have been made, and we are no longer like we were; our identity is being changed. The devil comes to steal, kill, and destroy us, but Jesus came to give life and life more abundantly. The devil has an identity that he wants you to continue in, and that is the old man...the old you. Jesus has brought each of us out of so much darkness and has made us a new creation. Colossians 1:13 tells us that, "He has delivered us from the power of darkness and conveyed us into the kingdom of His Son of His love."

Christ calls us a new creation, saints, and sons and daughters of God. Why listen to anything else? Everytime the devil tries to label you something you are not, tell him who you really are in Jesus' name!

Make this declaration today: "I have decided to live in my Christ-given identity. I will not listen to the lies of the enemy. My old self died with Christ, and I am a new creation. Old things have passed away, and all things have become new. I will no longer be sin-conscious, but righteous-conscious.

Thought and Reflection:

1. Think about who you use to be, the old "labels" that you had.

   Now, know that as a born-again believer, you are no longer any of those labels. Don't let the devil or anyone else beat you up. Do not be sin-conscious, but righteous-conscious.

   You have died with Christ (Rom. 6:6; Gal.2:20), been buried with Christ (Rom. 6:4), and have been raised with Christ (Eph. 2:5, 6; Col. 2:12). You need to, "reckon yourselves to be dead to sin, but alive to God in Christ Jesus our Lord" (Rom. 6:11).

NOTES

DAY 28

"I Have Decided to Allow the Holy Spirit to Work Fully in my Life."

But the Helper, the Holy Spirit, whom the Father will send in My name, He will teach you all things, and bring to your remembrance all things that I said to you.

John 14:26

The Holy Spirit has many operations in our lives. Today, we will walk through each of the operations that Scripture teaches us. Each operation shows us the Father's will for our lives. Remember also, that Scripture tells us not to quench the spirit of God (1 Thessalonians 5:19).

Advocates: The Holy spirit advocates on our behalf; He supports us, defends us, and pleads for us.

Convicts: The Holy Spirit convicts us of sin in our lives (John 16:8-9).

Draws us to Christ: The Holy Spirit draws us to salvation, and then closer to the Lord in our walk (John 16:14).

Teaches: The Holy Spirit is our teacher. He teaches us the Word of God; when we don't understand it, He brings clarity. He teaches us life lessons and how we should walk in this life (John 14:26).

Seals: The Holy Spirit seals us as God's people and assures us of our salvation (Ephesians 1:13).

Guides: The Holy Spirit guides us into all truth. He leads us in our everyday steps if we allow Him. He will be your GPS that will never lead you astray (John 16:13).

Intercedes: The Holy Spirit helps us in our weaknesses. He prays for us. Even when we don't know it, He is making intercession to God on our behalf. Have you ever wondered why all of a sudden you had the strength to do something, and you didn't know where it came from? (Romans 8:26).

Empowers: The Holy Spirit empowers us to do what God has called us to do. He provides supernatural strength and sustainability when we have none left on our own.

This is how God empowers His people—through the working of the Holy Spirit. It is, "not by might, nor by power, but by My Spirit, says the Lord" (Zech. 4:6). When you allow the Spirit to fully operate in your life, then there is no limit to what God can do through you and in you in Jesus' name.

<u>Make this declaration today</u>: I have decided to allow the Holy Spirit to work fully in my life. I will trust Him in every capacity that He serves.

Thought and Reflection:

1. Think of a time when you allowed the Holy Spirit to do His work in your life. How did you feel?

NOTES

NOTES

DAY 29

"I Have Decided to Walk in the Promises of God."

By faith Abraham obeyed when he was called to go out to the place which he would receive as an inheritance. And he went out, not knowing where he was going. By faith he dwelt in the land of promise as in a foreign country, dwelling in tents with Isaac and Jacob, the heirs with him of the same promise; for he waited for the city which has foundations, whose builder and maker is God.

Hebrews 11:8-10

As I was reading the Great Faith Chapter, as its called, in Hebrews Chapter 11, something stood out to me that I had never seen. In verses 8-10, it talks about how Abraham was in the Land of Promise as in a foreign country. Can it be that when we are walking in the promise of God, it will feel foreign, but at home at the same time?

Isn't that faith? Trusting God and being at peace with His promise, you may feel like you're operating in an uncertain terrain, but His promise keeps you going.

There "have been given to us exceedingly great and precious promises" (2 Peter 1:4). God is telling us to trust His promise, even when we are called to something foreign that we don't know. His promise is our road map. By faith, follow the promises of God, and you will birth amazing things in your life.

Make this declaration today: "I have decided to walk in the promises of God. God cannot lie, so every promise that He has made is guaranteed and belongs to me.

Thought and Reflection:

1. Maybe you are in uncertain terrain right now: a new job, school, relationship, and possibly made a move to another city. Begin listing the uncertain terrain in your life today.

   It may feel foreign, and you may even wonder what you are doing; but remember, if it was the promise of God that led you there you will be just fine.

NOTES

_____

_____

_____

_____

NOTES

DAY 30

"I Have Decided to Salt the Earth."

You are the salt of the earth; but if the salt loses its flavor, how shall it be seasoned? It is then good for nothing but to be thrown out and trampled underfoot by men. You are the light of the world. A city that is set on a hill cannot be hidden. Nor do they light a lamp and put it under a basket, but on a lampstand, and it gives light to all who are in the house. Let your light so shine before men, that they may see your good works and glorify your Father in heaven.

Matthew 5:13-16

I was asked by a friend if I like sea salt or table salt. I quickly answered, "Sea salt." After answering the question, the Holy Spirit said, "What about spiritual salt?" Then I heard the Holy Spirit ask, "Do I salt the earth as much as I salt my food? This is something to think about. Jesus calls us the salt of the earth, but are we truly salting the earth? Salt preserves, sustains, and adds flavor to everything it's put on.

When I think about how salt preserves and sustains, I think about how we in the body of Christ do that to each other. We help sustain and preserve each other through prayer, Bible study, communion, and fellowship with each other.

When I think about flavor, I think about food. I remember a dish I ordered at a small restaurant in the mountains of North Carolina that just hit me with explosive flavor. I still talk about that burrito. My point is this: when people first meet you, are you leaving them with a good flavor in their mouth or a bad one? You have to know how to season others lives so that you can leave a lasting impression on them, and that they will want more. Our saltiness should point them to Jesus, who is the source of our salt.

Make this declaration today: "I have decided to live as the salt of the earth. By the grace of God, everything that I say and do, I will do it as salt. I will live my life in order to preserve, sustain, and flavor everyone that I meet today."

Thought and Reflection:

> Paul encouraged the Colossians to, "Let your speech always be with grace, seasoned with salt, that you may know how to answer each one" (Col. 4:6).

1. Are there situations in your life that you need to be seasoned? Or maybe you missed out in salting someone else's life?

   Write your feelings and how you can improve; be transparent.

NOTES

_____

_____

_____

_____

NOTES

DAY 31

"I Have Decided to Apply Biblical Teachings to my Life."

Now to Him who is able to do exceedingly abundantly above all that we ask or think, according to the power that works in us.

Ephesians 3:20

Well friends, we have come to the end of this 31-day journey, but it is definitely not the end of decisions in our walk though. Seek the Lord's guidance every day, and He will never lead you down the wrong path. I believe that when you apply these simple decisions to your life, you will see great change, more joy, and more fulfillment in your life.

My earnest prayer is that this has been a thought-provoking journey and that it has brought you closer and stronger in the Lord Jesus. He will do above and beyond anything we could ever ask or think!

Make this declaration today: "I have decided to zero in upon the declarations that I have made this past month. By the grace of God, I will continue to grow in them, that I might glorify God in my life and lead others to Christ."

Thought and Reflection:

1. Take this day and reflect on how you are going to apply each of these topics to your life. What days do you excel at the most? What days do you really need to focus on and improve?

2. What have you learned from this devotional? Reflect and write everything that you received.

NOTES

_____

_____

_____

_____

NOTES

For His Glory Writing Co.
forhisglorywritingco@gmail.com